The Sto

Dorset

by Robert Westwood

Inspiring Places Publishing
2 Down Lodge Close
Alderholt
Fordingbridge
Hants.
SP6 3JA

ISBN 978-0-9955964-9-8
© Robert Westwood 2021
All rights reserved

JURASSICCOAST
QUALITY
BUSINESS

Contents

Introduction   3

Dorset Through Geological Time   4

The Ice Ages   10

The Jurassic Coast   13

Prehistoric and Ancient Dorset   14

The Dark Ages   20

Early Medieval   22

The Seventeenth Century Onwards   26

Dorset and the Sea   33

Some famous people of Dorset   37

Looking towards the village of Cranborne.

Introduction

Dorset combines a beautiful landscape and coastline with a fascinating natural and cultural history. A variety of sedimentary rocks dating from the Jurassic Period beginning around 200 million years ago to very much more recent strata only a few million years old, have been shaped into rolling hills, dramatic escarpments and fertile vales. The rocks are exposed along Dorset's spectacular coastline, most of which lies within the Jurassic Coast World Heritage Site. The geology and geography have had a profound impact on human habitation. The rich soils of the lowland areas have supported an agricultural economy for thousands of years and the Chalk downlands, originally heavily forested, have provided grasslands ideal for raising sheep and cattle. Iron Age man used many of Dorset's hills to build fortified settlements and natural harbours such as Poole and Christchurch have provided trading opportunities since ancient times. Although not especially rich in other natural resources, Portland and Purbeck stone has been quarried since Roman times.

Ancient remains are littered across Dorset; Neolithic henges, stone circles, Bronze Age burial barrows and Iron Age hillforts are all to be seen. Medieval castles, abbeys, manor houses and grand estates all have stories to tell. Pirates and smugglers have made use of the beaches and coves along the coast and Dorset has played its part in two world wars, perhaps most famously in 1944 when thousands of troops embarked from Dorset harbours to France on D-Day. This book will provide you with a brief overview of Dorset's wonderful story and hopefully encourage you to visit its many natural and cultural treasures, and perhaps delve a little more deeply into its history.

The Iron Age hillfort of Hod Hill.

Dorset Through Geological Time

Although the Earth is around 4.5 billion years old, most rocks we see on the surface were formed less than 500 million years ago. This is because the Earth's crust is constantly being recycled; oceans form and are squeezed out of existence, mountains are uplifted and eroded away and the continents are shifting position. The story of the rocks that have been shaped into the beautiful county of Dorset begins about 200 million years ago, the start of the geological period known as the Jurassic. Leading up to this period the Earth had witnessed an unusual, but not previously unknown, configuration of the continents; they were all joined together in one huge landmass, labelled Pangaea by geologists. The interior of this giant continent had largely been baking hot desert, and Devon's red rocks derive from this environment. As Pangaea began to break up at the start of the Jurassic, new marine environments were created, many that soon teemed with life. Clays, limestones and sandstones were deposited in these seas and in river deltas and coastal lagoons – for land was never far away from what would eventually be Dorset. The Cretaceous Period followed the Jurassic and again the sea level fluctuated before the great Chalk Sea covered most of southern England and the familiar white rock was deposited. Shortly after the Chalk came the end of the Cretaceous and also the end of the Mesozoic Era, the time zone that defines the Jurassic Coast (it includes

Below: The Jurassic Coast at Clavell's Hard near Kimmeridge. The rocks here are from the Kimmeridge Clay series and contain many marine fossils.

Above: Kimmeridge Bay; hard limestone layers form these ledges stretching out into the bay and make the waters hazardous for shipping.

the Triassic, Jurassic and Cretaceous periods). This division is not arbitrary, it marks the great extinction of many of the species that had thrived in the Jurassic seas, including the dinosaurs and the ammonites. Following this, Dorset saw many fluctuations of sea level as the Earth's crust prepared itself for another bout of mountain building as Africa moved towards Europe. Clays, sands and a few limestones formed in the shallow seas and river deltas and the continental collision that raised the Alpine mountain chain propagated peripheral ripples that gently buckled the sedimentary strata of Dorset.

This very short geological history will help us understand the nature of the rocks that have been sculpted into the landscape of Dorset. They are all sedimentary rocks, no volcanic or igneous rocks are to be found here.

The oldest rocks are in west Dorset, where the Lower Jurassic clays form fertile vales and the harder limestones and sandstones hills and ridges. The Chalk once spread across all this area but subsequent erosion has left it covering much of the middle of the county where it forms a gently curving upland. Its western and northern margins form spectacular escarpments, with many fine viewpoints overlooking the Jurassic vales. In the east of the county we see the largely clays and sandstones of the Cenozoic Era that followed the great extinction. They form a low, relatively flat landscape that includes the shallow basin of Poole Harbour.

We can now look into a little more detail at the various distinct regions of Dorset and appreciate how their character has been shaped by their underlying geology.

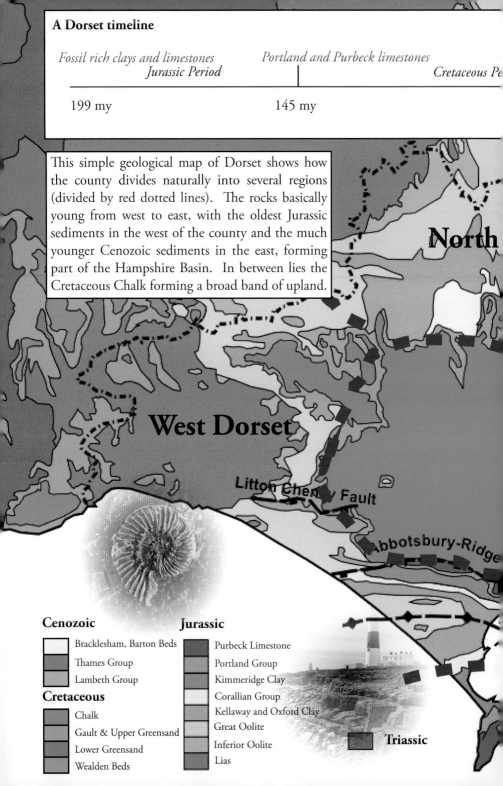

A Dorset timeline

Fossil rich clays and limestones
Jurassic Period

Portland and Purbeck limestones

Cretaceous Pe

199 my   145 my

This simple geological map of Dorset shows how the county divides naturally into several regions (divided by red dotted lines). The rocks basically young from west to east, with the oldest Jurassic sediments in the west of the county and the much younger Cenozoic sediments in the east, forming part of the Hampshire Basin. In between lies the Cretaceous Chalk forming a broad band of upland.

North

West Dorset

Litton Cheney Fault

Abbotsbury-Ridge

Cenozoic

	Bracklesham, Barton Beds
	Thames Group
	Lambeth Group

Cretaceous

	Chalk
	Gault & Upper Greensand
	Lower Greensand
	Wealden Beds

Jurassic

	Purbeck Limestone
	Portland Group
	Kimmeridge Clay
	Corallian Group
	Kellaway and Oxford Clay
	Great Oolite
	Inferior Oolite
	Lias

Triassic

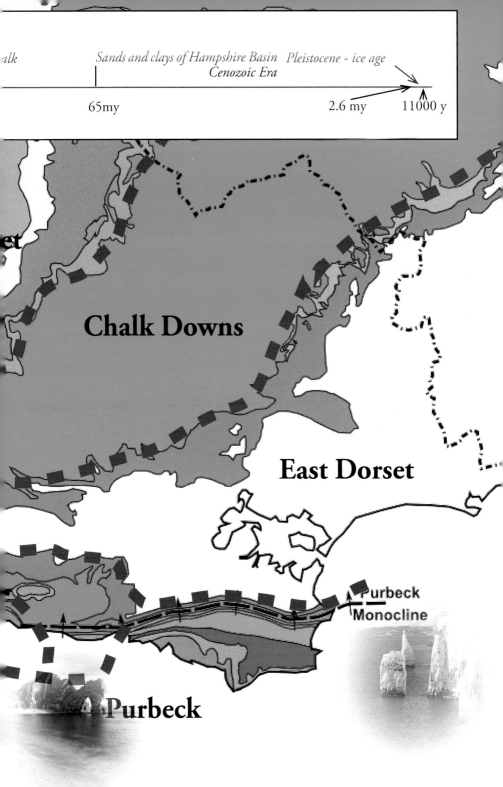

Chalk | Sands and clays of Hampshire Basin   Pleistocene - ice age

Cenozoic Era

65my   2.6 my   11000 y

Chalk Downs

East Dorset

Purbeck
Monocline

Purbeck

Above: Jurassic clays, shales and limestones at Lyme Regis.

West Dorset

The clays and limestones of the early Jurassic were followed by more wide-spread and persistent limestone deposition, a combination that has resulted in the wonderful rolling countryside, dotted with isolated hills and prominent ridges. On the coast we see the fossil rich clays exposed in Lyme Bay while harder sandstones form the magnificent cliffs at West Bay and Burton Bradstock. The Jurassic clays are interbedded with harder bands of limestone and most contain many fossils. The cliffs here are prone to collapse and it is the frequent cliff falls that reveal the fossils for enthusiastic collectors.

The Chalk Downs

Spread over the middle of the county is a layer of Chalk, often hundreds of feet thick. This forms a gently undulating countryside with large fields that once held hundreds of thousands of sheep. Nowadays the farming is more mixed. Several shallow valleys cut the Chalk Downs and small dry valleys are common (see page 11). The escarpments where the Chalk finishes provide some of Dorset's finest scenic landscapes. The

A dry valley near Durdle Door.

Chalk is a form of limestone, a rock composed almost entirely of calcium carbonate. This comes from microscopic coccolithophores, a type of phytoplankton which reproduce in huge numbers in warm seas. These tiny organisms protect themselves with intricately shaped calcite shields which they periodically shed. Billions of these drift to the bottom of the sea, forming a thick ooze. It is this that eventually turned to the familiar white rock. The Chalk formed in the Cretaceous Period, a time when the Earth's climate was much warmer than today. Sea levels rose inundating much of the continental landmass and creating shallow inland seas where it is thought much of the Chalk was deposited. These conditions must have been stable for millions of years to enable microscopic organisms to form rock layers hundreds of feet thick.

Chalk can also be found forming a ridge bounding the Isle of Purbeck in the west of the county. It is worth pointing out that the Chalk strata here lie tilted almost vertical, hence the narrow ridge – we see the edge of the strata. Elsewhere the Chalk strata lie horizontal or almost so, and therefore cover a large area. The tilting is due to the Alpine folding mentioned before.

North Dorset
The escarpment at the northern edge of the Chalk uplands looks over the Vale of Blackmore, a rich agricultural region underlain by Middle Jurassic clays, silts

Above: Chalk cliffs and stacks off Handfast Point between Studland and Swanage.

and sandstones with some bands of limestone. This fertile vale is drained by rivers flowing roughly north-eastwards into the River Stour.

East Dorset
Dorset east of the Chalk and north of the Isle of Purbeck is part of a geological region known as the Hampshire Basin. The rocks are largely sands and clays of Palaeogene age (younger than the Chalk) which have been folded into a very broad syncline (a downward bend). The clays can provide fertile soils while the sands gave rise to what were once extensive heathlands.

The Isles of Purbeck and Portland
Although we meet familiar Jurassic and Cretaceous sediments here, their structure is rather unique. While the Chalk to the north lies relatively flat or dipping

The rock strata at **Kimmeridge**, mostly shales and limestones, date from the Upper Jurassic around 150 million years ago. They were deposited in a fairly deep, tropical sea and conditions at the bottom were anoxic (with little or no oxygen), probably reflecting a sea with poor circulation. The upper waters teemed with life, ammonites and large marine reptiles among the many species present. The sediments that collected at the bottom of this sea were consequently rich in organic matter. The lack of oxygen meant that this matter did not oxidise, and when the resulting sediments are buried deeply under other strata this organic content turns to oil. It is these layers under the North Sea that have given us the large oil and gas deposits there. Efforts have been made to extract oil from the rocks at Kimmeridge, but in one attempt the lamp oil smelled so badly it was abandoned. It is the high organic content in the shales here that give them their dark grey/black colour.

gently southwards, here it rises to near vertical which, as we have seen, results in it presenting as a relatively narrow ridge. The older Cretaceous and Jurassic layers underneath have been folded to near vertical too before flattening out to dip gently southwards. If you find this difficult to imagine, picture the Portland and Purbeck limestones at Lulworth Cove dipping steeply, then the same limestones lying relatively flat to the south of the Isle of Purbeck and dipping gently southwards on the Isle of Portland.

The Ice Ages

The landscape of what is now Dorset began to evolve during the Cenozoic Era that followed the end of the Mesozoic. As we have seen, this was a time when the sediments deposited were mainly from large rivers and river deltas with some marine sediments when the sea transgressed. We might think of this time as one of increasing tectonic activity (earth movements) leading up to the

Kimmeridge beach.

Stair Hole, Lulworth.

Above: The almost circular cove at Lulworth. At the entrance to the cove are the steeply dipping Portland and Purbeck limestones. The Chalk forms the rear of the cove.

great Alpine mountain building episode and resulting in 'Dorset' being uplifted and the folding of strata we see in places like the Isle of Purbeck and Lulworth Cove. The covering of the more recent sediments began to be eroded; older and harder rock strata like the Chalk and Jurassic limestones formed hills, plateaus and escarpments and rivers, originating from spring lines below the Chalk and limestones, flowed typically eastwards or south-eastwards to the sea.

As the Cenozoic Era progressed the climate began to cool, a process that culminated in three Ice Ages during the last 1.5 million years. Dorset was never covered by ice sheets or glaciers, but permafrost, winter snow fields on the higher ground, fluctuations in sea level and an increase in the flow and power of rivers have all left their mark on the landscape. In interglacial periods and warmer summer months swollen rivers carried large amounts of sand and gravel forming terraces along such rivers as the Frome, Piddle and Stour. Today some of these deposits are of economic importance. Bournemouth Airport is built on a gravel terrace. The succession of glacial and interglacial periods caused great sea level changes. Raised beaches, for example, can be seen on Portland, indicating times when the sea level was much higher. At the end of the last Ice Age when the sea level again rose, the wide valley of the River Solent was flooded forming Poole Harbour and cutting off the Isle of Wight from the mainland. The Chalk is today cut by many dry valleys which were probably formed by rivers running over chalk made impermeable by permafrost.

The almost circular cove at **Lulworth** is one of the treasures of the Jurassic Coast. A gap has been eroded in the Portland and Purbeck limestones that face the sea, allowing it to erode the softer sands and clays behind at a relatively fast rate, scouring out the cove. It is perhaps natural to assume the sea created the gap in the limestones, but it was in fact the little stream that tumbles gently down through the village into the western side of the cove. At the end of the last ice age, as ice sheets to the north of Dorset began to melt, rivers became swollen. The little stream was then a powerful river; the sea level was lower and the gradient therefore steeper. It was this that broke through the limestones and allowed the sea to subsequently form the beautiful cove.

Neighbouring **Durdle Door** is perhaps equally famous. This spectacular arch in the steeply dipping Portland and Purbeck limestones has been formed by the erosive power of the sea, exploiting relatively weak planes along joints in the rocks. Joints typically form in rocks due to tensional stresses, usually when strata are folded. The Portland and Purbeck layers were gently folded during the same earth movements that formed the mountains of the Alps. The 'blocky' appearance of the limestones is due to the two sets of joints that have dominated the erosion of the arch. The limestone stacks forming a line west of Durdle Door reveal where the Portland and Purbeck strata once extended and where perhaps earlier arches were once created.

Durdle Door.

The Jurassic Coast

England's first natural World heritage Site was awarded its status in 2001. The rocks along this coast record 185 million years of Earth's history, from around 250 to 65 million years ago. This is known as the Mesozoic Era, comprising three 'periods', the Triassic, Jurassic and Cretaceous. The Dorset section of the Jurassic Coast stretches from the border with Devon to Studland and comprises rocks from the Jurassic and Cretaceous periods. At the start of the Mesozoic Era life on Earth was beginning to recover from a mass extinction. For much of the era the part of the world that is now Dorset was covered by warm shallow seas or was land with the ocean never far away. The sedimentary rocks that formed in these environments contain numerous fossils that record the many wonderful species that evolved and thrived there. Dinosaurs dominated the land while large marine reptiles and ammonites were prominent in the seas. Fossils of marine species are common at places like Lyme Regis and Charmouth while fossils of land species, although rarer, are found on the Isle of Purbeck in the Purbeck limestone which was formed in shallow coastal lagoons where dinosaurs once roamed amongst the luxuriant swamps. At Keates Quarry over one hundred footprints of giant, plant eating dinosaurs can be seen. At the end of the era another mass extinction occurred, possibly initiated by the impact of a large meteorite. The rocks along the Jurassic Coast are continually being eroded, revealing more fossils from this unique era in the history of life on Earth.

Below: The Jurassic Coast at Charmouth.

Prehistoric and Ancient Dorset

It is thought that the first modern humans, homo sapiens sapiens, arrived in Britain about fifteen thousand years ago, pursuing a hunter/gatherer existence on the frozen landscape. Around 8000 BP (before present) the climate began to warm up, Britain finally became an island as the land bridge across the Channel was breached and forests began to grow on the Chalk uplands. This is the time known as the Mesolithic or Middle Stone Age and the first known settlement site in Dorset, on Portland Bill, dates from this time. Another Mesolithic site has been found on Dog House Hill near Charmouth but it is not until the Neolithic or New Stone Age (beginning around 6000 BP) that Dorset presents us with evidence of considerable settlement. These people, it seems, were farmers rather than hunter/gatherers, adopting a more sedentary lifestyle than previous cultures. It is still uncertain how much this change was due to migration from the continent or the adoption of a different way of life by the native population. They had a considerable effect on Dorset's landscape, clearing much of the forest cover from the uplands and creating large areas of grassland. They also left many monuments, chambered tombs, stone circles, causewayed camps and even more enigmatic structures like the Dorset Cursus, a seven mile long avenue of earth banks and ditches that may have had some sort of ceremonial purpose. Hambledon Hill in east Dorset was once the site of a causewayed camp. A large cemetery and remains suggesting feasting excavated there perhaps indicate a ceremonial function rather than a permanent settlement.

Following the Neolithic was the Bronze Age; as the name suggests this was a time of more sophisticated

Rawlsbury Camp, Iron Age hillfort.

technology. The Bronze Age people are often known as 'Beaker' people from the ubiquitous pottery drinking vessel they used. They arrived here around 4000 BP, DNA evidence suggests an ancestry from the Eurasian steppes. Their way of life was probably not dissimilar to the native population they joined; ceremonial sites continued to be used. They left very many round burial barrows, mainly to be seen today on hills and ridges, particularly the Chalk uplands. We don't know if these were favoured locations or whether farming has obliterated those that were built on lower ground, but it seems likely that they would have farmed the fertile vales, except perhaps where there were heavy clay soils. Evidence of a major Bronze Age settlement has been found at Bestwall Quarry, Wareham; a site also with evidence of earlier Neolithic habitation.

Around 2800 BP is generally considered to be the onset of the Iron Age, again reflecting a development in technology; the use of iron tools and weapons. When the Romans came they described a number of tribes that inhabited different regions; Dorset was where the Durotriges lived. This is a Roman name; the Durotriges left no written records and even the coins they produced in the late Iron Age bore no written inscriptions. It is likely they were initially quite a disparate number of settlements who later formed a loose collaboration. The Romans regarded them as Celtic people and it is still not clear to what extent invasion, migration or gradual diffusion led to them being the domi-

nant group. The Celtic tribes produced no huge ritual or ceremonial sites but seemingly concentrated on organising and managing the land. They did, however, leave what are Dorset's most prominent ancient monuments, hillforts. These are to be found on hills and ridges throughout the county, many in spectacular and beautiful locations. The earliest hillforts were built about 2600 BP and their preponderance in Dorset suggests a densely populated landscape. Iron Age settlements undoubtedly covered much of Dorset's fertile vales and uplands, and the hillforts may have pro-

Below top: Three Bronze Age burial barrows near the Iron Age fort of Badbury Rings.
Bottom: Kingston Russell Neolithic stone circle.

vided places of refuge in times of danger for those living without their ramparts. In recent years a large Iron Age settlement, big enough to be called a 'town' has been discovered on open Chalk country near the village of Winterborne Kingston.

In 43 AD the Roman general Vespasian led his legion in the conquest of southern Britain, subduing the Britons in their hillforts one by one. The roughly four hundred years of relative peace that followed resulted in substantial population growth, while improved farming technology such as heavier ploughs enabled even more land to be cultivated. Lower land and river valleys were largely used for growing crops with valley sides and higher ground being used for pasture; a pattern that lasted well into medieval times. Although no grand buildings survive from Roman times they have left a number of intriguing remains. Ackling Dyke on Bottlebush Down near Cranborne

One of the largest hillforts in Western Europe, **Maiden Castle**, south of Dorchester, was started around 600 BCE. Although there was a decline in its population around 100 BCE it was still an important centre when the Romans invaded in 43 AD. Much has been made of discoveries during excavations in the 1930s by Sir Mortimer Wheeler. These included a number of human remains around one of the entrances; with one skeleton still with a Roman 'ballista' bolt embedded in its spine (on display in the Dorset Museum, Dorchester). It was assumed the remains came from a siege of the hillfort although this is not now thought to be the case. Nevertheless, it is clear the unfortunate man with the bolt in his back died in some sort of armed conflict, we are just not sure where this was.

Below: The massive ramparts at Maiden Castle, scene of a battle in 43 AD?

is perhaps the best preserved Roman road in southern England, while a clear outline of a Roman aqueduct follows the contours of the hillside at Poundbury, Dorchester. Also at Dorchester is the remains of a Roman town house, complete with mosaics and hypocaust. Archaeologists have found evidence of many Roman villas across the county, suggestive of a prosperous agricultural community.

Roman Dorchester developed after the conquest of nearby Maiden Castle in 43 AD, possibly as a legionary fort initially. The town soon became a regional centre; a regular street plan was laid out and Dorchester or 'Durnovaria', as it may have been called, was an important market centre for things such as Purbeck 'marble' and local potteries. Remains of the Roman era are still visible around Dorchester; as well as the town house

and aqueduct mentioned already there is a small section of the once impressive town walls and Maumbury Rings, a Neolithic henge monument which became a Roman amphitheatre.

The aqueduct at Poundbury.

Maumbury Rings.

The Roman Town House.

Dorset's Iron Age Hillforts

Iron Age hillforts occupy many of Dorset's finest viewpoints. Thirty-five have been recorded in the county; they began to be built around 2500 BP and were occupied for about 600 years by Iron Age people from a tribe known as the Durotriges. Some were simple affairs with one ditch and rampart, others were much more elaborate with three or four. Visit one of the larger ones such as Maiden Castle (see page 16) or Hambledon Hill and you will appreciate what a huge effort it must have taken to construct these. Defence was clearly one motive for building these forts but it is also speculated that status might have been another, with competing chieftains trying to outdo their neighbours.

A number of the sites were previously occupied by Bronze Age and Neolithic peoples. On Hambledon Hill for example there is evidence of a Neolithic 'causewayed camp' and many hillforts have Bronze Age round barrows. After the Roman conquest some were used by the invaders; the north-west corner of Hod Hill was used for a Roman fort. They would once have been crowded with people and livestock with numerous round, thatched huts.

There is much debate about their fate during the Roman conquest, evidence of 'battles' at some has been questioned; the presence of numerous ballista bolts found around what was once an Iron Age hut on Hod Hill has been interpreted as a concerted attack on the home of the chieftain but others have claimed this is more easily explained as target practice when the Romans were in occupation. There is no doubt that, after the conquest, the hillforts fell out of use, although there is evidence that some were reoccupied during the 'Dark Ages' after the Romans left.

Eggardon Hill and inset, Badbury Rings.

The Dark Ages

The time between the Roman withdrawal from Britain and the establishment of a stable Anglo-Saxon system of government has long been an enigmatic puzzle for historians. For Dorset this is perhaps particularly true. For example, excavations at what was a substantial Roman villa near Puddletown suggested that the villa remained in use for at least a century after the Roman withdrawal in 410 AD; hardly indicative of a collapse of social order that the name 'Dark Ages' is often thought to imply. On the Dorset/Hampshire border is an earthwork known as Bokerley Dyke; originally built in the Bronze or early Iron Age it was remodelled around 350 AD, probably as a defensive structure. We know that the Saxons landed near Southampton around 500 AD and won a decisive battle there, but the subsequent battle of Mount Badon, won by the Britons, seems to have halted the Saxon advance for a while. It seems likely that Dorset was not incorporated into the Saxon kingdom of Wessex for some time after that.

Archaeological evidence, particularly burials, indicates that during the seventh century there was growing Saxon influence in Dorset and by the time of King Ine (689 – 726) it was fully a part of the kingdom of Wessex. The Britons that they joined must have spoken a Celtic language but Dorset place names are almost wholly English in origin; those that derive from Celtic are usually describing landscape features. The relative peace of Saxon Dorset received a shock in 789 when the first recorded Viking raid took place on Portland. Three Viking ships landed on the shore there and King Beorhtric's reeve, who was in Dorchester, set out to meet them. The Saxons were wary of uninvited visitors and it is unlikely the meeting was convivial. The Vikings must have been nervous too and in the resulting clash, the Saxons were all killed. Viking raids along the coast continued and settlements on or near the coast must have lived in constant

Bokerley Dyke.

Above: The Saxon wall and the River Frome at Wareham.

fear. The Saxons built a stronghold at Corfe, later a formidable Norman castle, which controlled the main route through the chalk ridge from the Isle of Purbeck. After King Alfred had finally defeated the Danes he set about strengthening Dorset's defences, establishing fortified 'burghs' at Shaftesbury, Christchurch, Bridport and Wareham. Alfred's peace didn't last; after the 'golden age' of his grandson King Edgar, the young successor Edward was murdered at Corfe Castle on the orders of his stepmother (see page 28). Her son Ethelred (the Unready) became king and Viking attacks resumed and intensified. Peace was finally restored when the Dane Canute became king. Canute died in 1035 at Shaftesbury, possibly while on a pilgrimage to the aforementioned King Edward who was buried in the abbey there and subsequently canonised (see page 25).

In 875 AD Wareham was occupied by a large Viking army. After spending the winter there they left for Exeter and luckily for King Alfred and the people of Wessex, many of the 120 Viking ships were lost in a storm off Swanage, probably near Peveril Point. A monument on the seafront at Swanage commemorates this, but claims it as a great Saxon victory. Wareham was one of Alfred's fortified 'burghs' and the earthen banks that surround the town on three sides are the Saxon walls constructed on his orders. They were once topped with wooden palisades and towers. Wareham was protected on the south side by the River Frome. Today a pleasant walk can be had along the top of these ancient 'walls'.

Early Medieval

At the time of the Norman conquest Dorset was a relatively prosperous agricultural region with towns and villages that are largely still with us today. Duke William intended to consolidate his new kingdom through cooperation and Dorset may have escaped relatively unscathed had not a rebellion broken out in the South-West, centred around King Harold's mother. Some Saxons from Dorset supported the rebellion and William led his army to besiege Exeter, laying waste to a number of Dorset towns on his way.

Dorset saw further conflict in the twelfth century in the so-called 'Anarchy', the civil war between King Stephen and the Empress Matilda. By then the Normans had already built a number of castles in the county and Corfe Castle was besieged by Stephen when it was held by supporters of Matilda. Some of the Norman castles like those at Wareham and Dorchester have disappeared but several impressive fortifications still remain, notably Corfe and Sherborne. To secure their hold over the country the Normans also built many motte and bailey castles in manors that had been taken from their Saxon thegns and handed to Norman knights. Many of the earth mounds or baileys still remain in Dorset; a good example can be seen at Cranborne. The population of Dorset grew in the twelfth and thirteenth century as agriculture flourished and the quarrying of Purbeck marble added to the prosperity in that region. Along with prosperous manors were a number of wealthy abbeys such as those at Abbotsbury, Cerne Abbas and Shaftesbury. The manufacture of rope helped Bridport and the surrounding area flourish. The hinterland of the town was ideal for growing flax and hemp and the industry was given a huge boost when King John

Cranborne Castle.

The Norman castle in Sherborne was built in the early twelfth century for Roger de Caen, Bishop of Salisbury. Roger was Chancellor to Henry I and the second most powerful man in England. He ruled England while Henry was in France. The castle was really a fortified palace; it was confiscated by King Stephen after a siege there in the civil war between Stephen and Matilda. It remained in royal hands although was briefly returned to the church by Edward III. Sir Walter Raleigh fell in love with its setting and persuaded Elizabeth I to grant him the lease. He soon found the castle far from comfortable and had a new palace built in the grounds, 'new' Sherborne Castle. The old castle was the scene of a bitter siege in the English Civil War, in 1645. It was occupied by Royalists who held out for many days until the Parliamentarians of General Fairfax captured it.

ordered Bridport to make as many ropes as possible for the navy.

Early in the fourteenth century a colder climate cycle badly affected crops and there was widespread famine. Worse was to come in 1348 when the Black Death arrived in England, brought there by a merchant ship from Venice that docked at Weymouth. Within days people were dying in surrounding villages. Many villages were abandoned during this time and in the coming years; their remnants are to be found all over Dorset. The bad times

Old Sherborne Castle.

New Sherborne Castle.

Athelhampton House.

continued in the fifteenth century, but looking at Dorset's fine collection of medieval churches one might be inclined to think differently since many of them were rebuilt or had extensive and elaborate additions. Many of Dorset's wealthy families continued to prosper and sponsored the 'improvements' to their local parish churches. For example the Martyn family who built the lovely manor house at Athelhampton were responsible for the rebuilding of Puddletown church.

The economic landscape began to change in the late fifteenth century, with farming the principal factor. A modern visitor to this era might recognise familiar field patterns, but would undoubtedly be struck by the number of sheep in them. The trade in wool was proving extremely lucrative and most levels of society saw an improvement in their standard of living. It was sheep

farming that had led to the enclosure of much of the common land, often by the mutual consent of all involved. The sixteenth century saw great changes in the ownership of Dorset's agricultural land. The Dissolution of the Monasteries under Henry VIII resulted in the vast estates of the abbeys and priories passing to wealthy families and supporters of the king. Yeomen farmers were becoming increasingly prosperous and were able to buy their own farms.

Bingham's Melcombe's 14th C church.

Much of Dorset's rich agricultural land was once owned and managed by the many **abbeys and priories** that were to be found all over the county. Some had relatively small holdings but others grew very rich and governed extensive estates. All were taken over by the Crown in 1539 and many of their fine buildings were plundered for stone or left to gradually ruin. Fortunately some buildings were spared, like the wonderful abbey church at Sherborne which became the parish church. Others, such as Forde Abbey, became grand houses while some survive as enigmatic, often atmospheric, ruins. Many have interesting histories; Shaftesbury Abbey was founded by Alfred the Great in 888 who installed his daughter as abbess. It grew very rich after the remains of the Saxon King Edward 'the Martyr' were brought there, encouraging many pilgrims after Edward was canonised. The sparse remains are now part of a charming garden and are open to the public. Sherborne was founded in 998 and had St Aldhelm as its first bishop. Milton Abbey was founded by King Athelstan in 934 and again the lovely, but never finished, abbey church remains. Abbotsbury Abbey was founded in around 1030 by a steward of King Canute. It was largely destroyed in the Civil War and its lands granted to the Strangways family. Its magnificent fourteenth century tithe barn remains, together with remnants scattered around the village.

Shaftesbury Abbey.

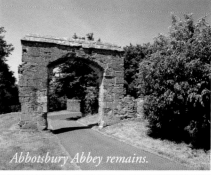

Abbotsbury Abbey remains.

Milton Abbey.

Abbot's Porch, Cerne Abbas.

The Seventeenth Century Onwards

The seventeenth century in England was blighted by the Civil War in the 1640s. Dorset witnessed a number of bloody encounters and its two major castles, Corfe and Sherborne were both ruined in the conflict. Both were Royalist strongholds and were eventually taken by the Parliamentarians, Corfe after two sieges where the defenders were famously commanded by the brave and determined Lady Bankes. Lyme Regis by contrast, was a Parliamentary stronghold and the scene of long and bitter

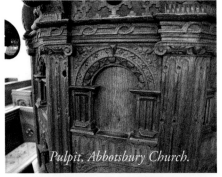

Pulpit, Abbotsbury Church.

fighting as it was besieged by a Royalist force led by Prince Maurice, nephew of King Charles. The town held out and remained in the hands of Parliamentarians, as did the town of Weymouth, also the scene of bitter fighting after Royalists, aided by sympathisers within the town, launched a surprise attack. They were initially able to capture the town and its two forts, but were later driven out by a counter attack.

A smaller skirmish at Abbotsbury has left a unique mark on this pretty village which was owned by the Royalist Strangways family. It was attacked by a force of Parliamentarians who eventually took the family house where the defenders had retreated. The fighting lasted six hours and at one point spread to the church. The pulpit there still has clearly defined holes left by musket balls.

The effect of the war on England's population was devastating. As well as casualties from battle and inevitable disease, the opposing armies often

Lyme Regis Harbour.

Hambledon Hill.

stripped local communities of horses and provisions. Groups of so-called 'Clubmen' arose in parts of the country, challenging both sides in an effort to protect their homes and livelihoods. Several thousand Dorset Clubmen gathered on Hambledon Hill in 1645 and were confronted by a force led by Oliver Cromwell. The Clubmen were no match for the trained soldiers and the fighting was brief. Around sixty Clubmen were killed and many taken prisoner. They were held overnight and released after a stern lecture by Cromwell.

After the Civil War peace returned to Dorset but was shattered again during the reign of King James when James, Duke of Monmouth, an illegitimate son of Charles II, landed at Lyme Regis in 1685 with a group of followers and a plan to overthrow the Protestant King James. Not enough people rallied to his cause however and his force was soundly beaten at the Battle of Sedgemoor in Somerset. Brutal reprisals followed and the infamous Judge Jeffreys conducted his 'Bloody Assizes', including sessions at Dorchester and Lyme Regis. Twelve men were hanged on Monmouth Beach, Lyme Regis where the ill-fated landing occurred.

In 1686 a secret meeting took place at Charborough House near Bere Regis that began the planning for the 'Glorious Revolution' that led to the overthrow of James II and put William of Orange and his wife Mary jointly on the throne.

The eighteenth and nineteenth centuries saw the modern Dorset rural landscape emerge. Enclosure of common fields continued, but this had largely been complete anyway in Dorset. The big change was the enclosure of the Chalk downland and the Dorset

Corfe Castle is built on a natural, isolated hill formed by two streams cutting through the Chalk ridge (they were once much larger). The Saxons first built a castle on it and it was here in 978 that the young King Edward was murdered, probably on the orders of his step-mother Aelfthryth. He was succeeded by her son Ethelred (the Unready) who was subsequently forced to pay large sums of money to keep the Danes and Vikings away. After the conquest the Normans built a stone castle which was gradually enlarged through the centuries. It became a favourite hunting destination for King John. It was besieged by King Stephen in the civil war with Henry I's daughter Matilda, and again in the English Civil War when it was taken and ruined by Parliamentarians, following a long siege famous for the brave defence organised by **Lady Mary Bankes**, whose husband Sir John Bankes was away and later killed fighting for the king. An initial attempt to take the castle in 1643 was thwarted when Lady Mary and her maids opened fire with cannons. The attackers returned but not before a small band of reinforcements had reached the castle. The following siege lasted six weeks after which the Parliamentarians were forced to retire. They returned again the following year with a larger force and again Lady Mary organised and led a brave defence. She was finally forced to submit when one of her own officers betrayed her and secretly led a party of Roundheads into the castle. The Parliamentarians, impressed by her bravery, let her leave unharmed with the seal and keys to the castle. After the Restoration King Charles II restored the estate to the Bankes family although the castle was no longer habitable. They built a new home, Kingston Lacy, on their land near Wimborne.

The Blackmore Vale from Rawlsbury Camp.

heathland, mainly for sheep. It was in this period that the large, regular fields we see today on the Chalk upland were created. In the early eighteenth century Daniel Defoe completed his "tour through the whole island of Great Britain". Writing about Dorset he said that the downs around Dorchester were "exceedingly pleasant" and had been told that there were six hundred thousand sheep within six miles of the town. He noted that "when I viewed the country round, I confess I could not but incline to believe it."

Life was generally hard for the rural poor; most were labourers or small tenant farmers with few rights. This was the age of widespread smuggling; crippling tax rises on goods like tea and brandy to pay for the many wars made for a lucrative trade. All levels of soci-ety were involved and few thought such activity immoral (see page 35). In contrast to the rural poverty, Dorset's great landowners continued to prosper and people with 'new' wealth also moved into the county. New mansions were built and existing ones improved and enlarged. In the early nineteenth century new mechanised farming techniques threatened the livelihood of the many labourers. Resentment grew and culminated in the "Captain Swing' riots of 1830. Farms were attacked and threshing machines destroyed. The authorities dealt with the rioters ruthlessly and shortly afterwards a group of labourers who formed an entirely legal Friendly Society to negotiate their pay were sentenced to deportation on trumped up charges. They gained immortality as the 'Tolpuddle Martyrs'.

The Tolpuddle Martyrs

Every year in July thousands gather in a small Dorset village to celebrate the actions, in 1834, of six local farm labourers. These men, like many others at the time, earned nine shillings a week and lived in terrible poverty with their families. The trade union movement was just beginning and unions were perfectly legal. Under the leadership of George Loveless, the six men met by the sycamore tree in the village centre and set about forming a union to protest about their pay. Local landowner James Frampton heard about this and, with memories of the French Revolution and the Swing riots fresh in his mind, was determined to stamp this out. The men swore an oath of secrecy and Frampton used this to bring a trumped up charge against the men; a law had been passed about such oaths, primarily to prevent naval mutinies. Frampton had managed to get a couple of informers inducted into the labourers' Friendly Society and acting on advice from the Home Secretary, Lord Melbourne, had the parish constable arrest the men. They were taken to Dorchester where they were tried by a jury few would consider impartial. Frampton himself and his son were both members of the jury!

The trial was over in two days, all six men were found guilty and sentenced to the maximum punishment - seven years transportation. They were taken in chains to prison hulks, old ships ready to be scrapped, where they were fettered with heavy irons. Along with hundreds of others they suffered a long, arduous voyage to Australia; disease was rampant due to the filthy conditions. Once there they were used as slaves to do heavy, manual work.

Back home word spread and anger grew over the men's treatment. In London it is thought around 100 000 marched to parliament to protest. It took time but in the end the King issued all a free pardon; George Loveless was the first to arrive home in June 1837. Only one of the Martyrs, James Hammett, settled back in Tolpuddle. The others were helped by public donations to set up farms in Essex, but continued pressure from wealthy landowners eventually forced them to emigrate to Canada, where they settled as farmers in Ontario.

The Tolpuddle Martyrs Museum.

Although much of Dorset's industrial activity was concerned with agriculture, the quarrying of Portland and Purbeck stone expanded in the nineteenth century partly due to the Victorian efforts to reshape much of London. Portland Stone was reckoned to be the world's best building stone and it was quarried along the coast of Purbeck and on the Isle of Portland itself. Most quarries were privately owned and worked by relatively small numbers of skilled craftsmen. Small cranes or 'whims' loaded the cut stone onto barges or ships. With the advent of the railways it became possible to work quarries in the north of Portland which were not directly on the coast.

Throughout the eighteenth and nineteenth centuries land ownership continued to be mostly in the hands of wealthy families who lived in grand estates, most of which continue to be in private hands, and some still with the same families. Owner of the most extensive estate was Augustus Pitt-Rivers at Rushmore on Cranborne Chase. He was responsible for the meticulous excavation of many ancient remains and is widely regarded as the father of modern archaeology. Another grand estate was that of the Earls of Shaftesbury at Wimborne St Giles.

In the twentieth century Dorset remained a largely agricultural county, although the rise in popularity of the seaside holiday led to the growth of Weymouth and Bournemouth as resorts. Until the eighteenth century Bournemouth was uninhabited heath-

Old quarry workings on Portland Bill.

land, and the coastline much favoured by smugglers to land their contraband. Dorset played its part in the two world wars. In 1914 the Grand Fleet assembled in Portland Harbour while in 1944 thousands of allied troops gathered all over the county in preparation for D-Day, with many embarking for France at Poole and Weymouth. Dorset's airfields were active throughout World War II, especially during the Battle of Britain, and the first paratroopers that landed in Normandy on June 6th, 1944 took off in their gliders from Tarrant Rushton airfield.

Dorset is still a largely rural county; it has no motorways and no city. Farming is still an important activity and with over 40% of the county an Area of Outstanding Natural Beauty and over eighty miles of the wonderful Jurassic Coast, it's no surprise that tourism is now a very important part of the county's economy.

Above top: Gold Hill, Shaftesbury and below, Forde Abbey, two of Dorset's popular tourist atttractions.
Below: The Cobb, Lyme Regis.

Dorset and the Sea

With around eighty-eight miles of coastline (excluding the shoreline of Poole Harbour) facing France across the English Channel, the sea has always been prominent in Dorset's history. Despite having what is reputedly the second largest natural harbour in the world in Poole Harbour, this coastline is rather lacking in natural harbours. There is the small but beautiful cove at Lulworth and the River Wey at Weymouth, but not much else; the harbours at Lyme Regis and West Bay are both artificial.

The Cobb at Lyme Regis seems to have been in existence in some form since the early fourteenth century and used to consist of wooden piles and boulders. Lyme's heyday was between about 1500 and 1700 when it traded with Europe, the Mediterranean, Africa and the Americas. Its business included, it has to be said, trade in slaves.

The floodplain of the River Brit has provided an ideal location for growing hemp. The Romans are thought to have introduced this and a rope making industry quickly followed. This became a major occupation in the time of King John who required vast amounts of rope to equip the navy. It has flourished ever since, developing into a net making industry as well and, in more modern times, using synthetic materials. There is no natural harbour near Bridport, the river estuary is prone to silting up, so the harbour at West Bay has been created by dredging and building harbour walls. The present harbour there dates from around 1740. You might be aware that, more recently, West Bay was the setting for the fictional

The harbour, West Bay.

'Broadchurch' of the television series.

West Bay marks the start of Chesil Beach, an eighteen mile long shingle storm beach that only reached its present form around 5000 years ago. At its eastern end it encloses the Fleet, a shallow brackish water lagoon that is home to the famous swannery at Abbostbury. Long associated with smuggling, thanks partly to the novel *Moonfleet* by J Meade Falkner, it was also the site where Barnes Wallis's 'bouncing bomb' was first tested during World War II.

Weymouth was originally two towns set either side of the estuary of the River Wey, Weymouth to the west and Melcombe Regis to the east. They became one borough in the sixteenth century on the orders of Elizabeth I. Melcombe Regis gained notoriety in 1348 when a merchant ship brought the Black Death to the town and subsequently the rest of England. Although it had always been an important port, its trade was declining in the eighteenth century as ships became bigger and its riverside quays became more and more unsuitable. Fortunately for the town its prosperity was ensured as it became a centre for privateers; pirates legalised by royal commission. In 1775 only 65 seamen were based in Weymouth, by 1810 that figure had risen to 2188. Alongside this business, Weymouth also prospered by developing as a resort following the rise in popularity of sea bathing. It attracted wealthy and influential visitors, culminating in 1789 with the arrival of a convalescing King George III. He returned to the town regularly, boosting Weymouth's growing tourist industry as he did so.

The old harbour, Weymouth.

Smuggling in the eighteenth and nineteenth centuries

In the eighteenth and early nineteenth centuries smuggling developed into a huge industry. Much of the Dorset coast was regularly used to land contraband, typically tea and brandy from France. Enclosures of common land and crippling taxation had left many desperately poor and there was little sympathy for the government. By 1783 it was estimated that nine out of ten families supported smuggling and every level of society was involved. For much of its history smuggling was relatively risk free with few 'Riding Officers' available to intercept the smuggling gangs. Things changed in the nineteenth century when the Coastguard was formed to patrol the coast, using many men from the army when war with France was finally over. The South West Coast Path was originally created to enable Coastguards to keep a watch on every cove and beach. Many places along the coast were used by the smugglers for a variety of reasons. Christchurch has an excellent harbour and is at the confluence of two rivers; ideal for quickly transporting goods inland. Bournemouth in the eighteenth century was just a barren wilderness of heathland where boats could be unloaded in secrecy with tracks leading inland all the way to Cranborne Chase. The photograph below shows Brandy Bay where, as its name suggests, kegs were landed on the beach and hauled up the cliffs on ropes. The cliffs provided excellent lookout stations for the smugglers.

Brandy Bay.

The Isle of Portland has long had a special character; very different from its near neighbour. Its surface rocks are the Portland and Purbeck limestones. The Portland in particular occurs in thick strata which slope gently southwards, making it relatively easy for the rock to be quarried on the southern shore and loaded into waiting ships. As mentioned before, it was the coming of the railways that enabled large quarries in the north of the isle to flourish, which they did until the early twentieth century. A naval base was established here in 1845 and convicts from Portland Prison were used to build the breakwater around the harbour. It was the largest man made harbour in the world and in 1914 the Grand Fleet sailed from here.

The limestone coast of Purbeck was another site where Portland Stone was quarried. It was loaded onto small boats by 'whims' (small cranes) and often rowed out to larger ships offshore. The town of Swanage became a major centre for the trade in the stone with ships loading from the town's pier. The Victorian entrepreneurs John Mowlem and nephew George Burt developed a thriving business supplying stone to London and contributed to the growth of Swanage as a prosperous trading town and subsequently a successful resort.

Below: The Fleet lagoon.
Bottom: Swanage.

Below: Looking down on Weymouth and Portland Harbour.

Today they join in one large conurbation but Bournemouth and Poole have very different histories. Just over two hundred years ago Bournemouth was a sandy stretch of coastline bordered by heathland. It was a Victorian soldier, Capt. Lewis Tregonwell who bought a piece of land there and built a villa for himself and his wife. The idea caught on and a town quickly developed. The town of Poole, built around the edge of its great harbour had been an important port for centuries, with settlement dating back to the Iron Age. The Romans used the harbour to bring in supplies for their invasion forces and in the Middle Ages Poole became prosperous through the trade in wool.

Both Poole and Weymouth saw thousands of soldiers embark for France on the night of 5th June, 1944. Poole shipbuilders built landing craft and other vessels. Ports like Poole and Portland are still involved in trade, but it is tourism that is the mainstay of the economy along the Dorset coast.

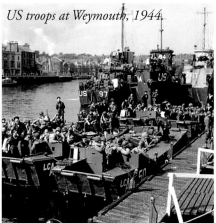

US troops at Weymouth, 1944.

Above: Dancing Ledge on Purbeck.

Some Famous People of Dorset

The following pages describe some of Dorset's most famous characters. There are, of course, many others of this county who have done remarkable things and whose legacies continue to inspire; we have already met the Tolpuddle Martyrs whose actions helped galvanise the Trade Unions movement, and the brave Lady Mary Bankes. The men and women I have chosen came from a variety of backgrounds; from royalty and aristocracy to the very humble. Some are perhaps more famous than others, but all have a fascinating story to tell. They are also all associated with places in Dorset well worth visiting, where it might be possible to learn more about their interesting lives.

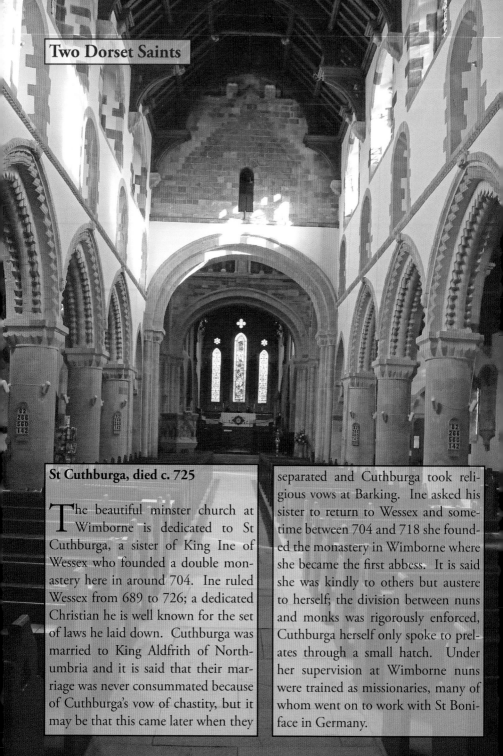

Two Dorset Saints

St Cuthburga, died c. 725

The beautiful minster church at Wimborne is dedicated to St Cuthburga, a sister of King Ine of Wessex who founded a double monastery here in around 704. Ine ruled Wessex from 689 to 726; a dedicated Christian he is well known for the set of laws he laid down. Cuthburga was married to King Aldfrith of Northumbria and it is said that their marriage was never consummated because of Cuthburga's vow of chastity, but it may be that this came later when they separated and Cuthburga took religious vows at Barking. Ine asked his sister to return to Wessex and sometime between 704 and 718 she founded the monastery in Wimborne where she became the first abbess. It is said she was kindly to others but austere to herself; the division between nuns and monks was rigorously enforced, Cuthburga herself only spoke to prelates through a small hatch. Under her supervision at Wimborne nuns were trained as missionaries, many of whom went on to work with St Boniface in Germany.

Inside Wimborne Minster.

St Wite, c. 9th century

There are said to be only two churches in England which hold the remains of a saint. One is Westminster Abbey where Edward the Confessor lies, the other is the church of St Candida and Holy Cross at Whitchurch Canonicorum in Dorset. Here, it is thought, lie the bones of Dorset's very own patron saint, St Wite (Candida is the Latin name). Her shrine is in the north transept and, when the stone reliquary was opened in 1850, was found to contain the bones of a small woman, and when opened again in 1900, an inscription was found saying (in Latin) "Here lie the bones of St Wite". She is a mysterious figure, one story associates her with a Saxon princess who lived as a hermit (or an-

choress) on the nearby coast and lit beacons for the safety of sailors. She was captured and tortured by Danish raiders (losing a finger) but managed to escape and warn villagers. She may have been later murdered. It is also possible she was a Breton saint. King Athelstan allowed people from Brittany to seek refuge in England and some brought sacred relics, among them, perhaps, those of St Gwen; Gwen is a Celtic name associated with white. However, this does not explain why the name of the village derives from the time of Alfred the Great who founded a church there. The present church was begun in the eleventh century and there have been many later additions and enlargements. In the Middle Ages it became a major centre of pilgrimage.

The figure of St Wite on the outside wall of the church.

Margaret Beaufort, 1443-1509

Margaret Beaufort was not born in Dorset but has strong links with the county. She was the daughter of John Beaufort, Duke of Somerset and Margaret Beauchamp. The Duke was the legitimised grandson of John of Gaunt, son of Edward III and held large estates in Dorset at Corfe, Kingston Lacy and Canford. The Duke and Duchess are buried in a tomb in Wimborne Minster. Kingston Lacy was originally part of a royal estate and was leased to John Beaufort by the king. The present house dates from the seventeenth century; the original one has long since vanished and it was here that Margaret spent much of her childhood. She was not allowed to remain a child for long however; at the request of King Henry VI Margaret was married to Edmund Tudor, Henry's half-brother while still only twelve years old. At the tender age of thirteen Margaret gave birth to a son, Henry, who would later become King Henry VII, the first of the Tudor sovereigns. Edmund died of the plague before Henry was born and Margaret married three more times; her second husband died in battle at the age of twenty-eight. Throughout the Wars of the Roses Margaret was close to those in power. Edmund Tudor had been a Lancastrian and Margaret was reputedly involved in several conspiracies against Richard III while Henry was in exile in France with his uncle. Margaret negotiated that Henry married Elizabeth, Edward IV's oldest daughter and heir to the throne following the deaths of the 'princes in the tower', something that Margaret has been linked with by many. Henry returned to England in 1485 to claim the throne, which he did after the Battle of Bosworth. She remained close to Henry throughout his reign and in her will set up a provision for a grammar school in Wimborne. Queen Elizabeth I confirmed this provision on the condition that it be named after her. Today the Queen Elizabeth School, Wimborne is still flourishing.

Kingston Lacy today.

Thomas Sydenham, 1624-1689

The tiny hamlet of Wynford Eagle near Dorchester sits in a fold of the Chalk downland. The manor house there was the birthplace of Thomas Sydenham, a man sometimes called the 'father of English medicine' or the 'English Hippocrates'. The Sydenhams were a wealthy Puritan family and when civil war broke out in 1642 William Sydenham and his five sons joined the side of Parliament. Thomas was the youngest and cut short his medical studies in strongly Royalist Oxford to join the Parliamentary cause. Three of the sons were to die in the fighting and their mother, Lady Sydenham, was killed in a most unsavoury fashion; a group of Royalist soldiers called at the family home and one of them murdered Mary Sydenham on the doorstep. The family had their revenge when one of the sons, Francis, recognised the culprit among Royalist soldiers near Poole. It is said that he and other cavalry officers chased the Royalists, caught up with them near Dorchester where Francis shot dead his mother's murderer.

After the war, Thomas continued his studies at Oxford and later Cambridge. He became disillusioned with the current medical methods, believing that careful, clinical observation of diseases was crucial for effective treatment. Sydenham successfully treated many patients and was held in high regard because of this but his emphasis on empirical methods made him unpopular with many other physicians of the day. It was only after his death that his ideas and work were fully appreciated.

Wynford Eagle and, inset, the manor house.

William and Clotilde Lawrence, 1791-1869 and 1792-1853

In the churchyard beside the ancient Norman church at Studland lies a grave that tells a remarkable story. Buried there are William and Clotilde Lawrence. They lived in this quiet village for over thirty years, managing the village inn, the site of which was near the present Bankes' Arms. That Clotilde was French, William English and the fact they married in 1815 might give a clue to the circumstances of their meeting. At that time William was a Serjeant of the 40th Regiment of Foot in Wellington's army. He was born in Briantspuddle and in his youth apprenticed to a builder in Studland. He may not have been treated well by his employer for he soon ran away to join the army - the start of a long and distinguished career. In 1805 he was fighting the Spanish in South America and from 1808 to 1812 he fought with Wellington in the Peninsular War against the French in Spain. There he took part in every major battle, including being part of the 'Forlorn Hope' (the initial frontal assault) at Badajuz where he was badly wounded. He followed Wellington to France where he saw action at Waterloo. It was in Paris after the battle that William met and fell in love with Clotilde Clairet. It seems she was running a stall selling garden produce outside William's barracks. They were given permission to marry and Clotilde followed William back to Britain. Discharge from the army did not follow immediately and the pair often had long walks to and from various postings. Once, after a visit to William's family in Briantspuddle they walked all the way back to Glasgow. William was discharged in Plymouth in 1821 and the pair walked back to Studland where they eventually set up in the Wellington Inn. They lived peacefully and happily here for many years; Clotilde died in 1853 and William survived for another sixteen years.

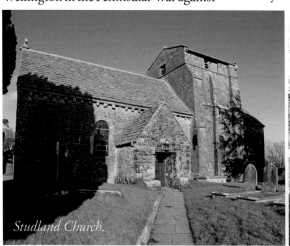

Studland Church.

The grave of Sgt. and Clotilde Lawrence

Mary Anning, 1799-1847

Mary Anning was born in Lyme Regis in 1799, a time when the science of geology had not really become established. However, as the nineteenth century progressed the idea of a vast geological time scale became more accepted and demand grew from museums and universities for more and more specimens of fossils. Mary's father was a carpenter but supplemented his income by selling 'curiosities' in a little shop. He sadly died when Mary was eleven and she and her brother decided to continue this business, having already become used to fossil hunting in the Jurassic cliffs of the town. In 1811 Mary uncovered the first full skeleton of an Ichthyosaur, a previously unknown marine reptile. She went on to make many more spectacular finds, including the first skeleton of a Plesiosaur, a strange, large, long-necked marine reptile. Mary's fame spread and she was consulted by many prominent scientists and collectors. She became good friends with Henry de la Beche, a pioneer geologist and palaeontologist who became the first president of the Geological Survey. De la Beche was a good artist and he had a sketch of his showing some of Mary's finds made into a print; this sold well and he donated the proceeds to Mary, who despite her fame, was still in financial difficulties. Although as a woman, Mary was not allowed to join the Geological Society, it did award her an annual grant in recognition of her work. Mary died in 1847 of breast cancer.

An ammonite, Monmouth Beach.

The Ammonite Pavement, Lyme Regis.

Monmouth Beach, Lyme Regis.

Thomas Hardy, 1840-1928

Thomas Hardy was born on June 2nd, 1840 in a small cottage in Higher Bockhampton near Dorchester. That cottage is now looked after by the National Trust and welcomes visitors to its simple interior and luxuriant cottage garden. Hardy's mother was educated and well-read, and undoubtedly contributed to her son's interest in literature. His formative years were spent in close contact with nature and the rural way of life, leaving an indelible influence on the young man. After school Hardy was apprenticed to an architect in Dorchester, moving to London when he was twenty-two to continue his training. After five years he returned to Dorset and completed his first novel, *The Poor Man and the Lady*, unpublished and now lost.

In 1870 Hardy met and fell in love with Emma Gifford on an architectural visit to Cornwall. They married in 1874 by which time Hardy had completed three more novels, published in serial form in popular magazines. His fourth, *Far From the Madding Crowd*, became a sensation and was successful enough to enable him to marry Emma and give up architectural work. Their marriage did not work out well and the pair became more and more estranged.

Clockwise from top left: Hardy's old school house at Lower Bockhampton, his grave at Stinsford, Stinsford Church and Max Gate, the house he designed himself.

Hardy's Cottage, Higher Bockhampton.

In 1885 they moved to Max Gate, a house near Dorchester that Hardy designed himself. Here he wrote four more novels, culminating in *Jude the Obscure*, a work that outraged Victorian sensibilities and caused Hardy to give up writing novels and concentrate on poetry, publishing over nine hundred poems in a thirty year period. Emma died in 1912 and Hardy, feeling a deep sadness and regret at his treatment of her, produced a collection "Poems 1912-1913", containing many beautiful verses.

Within two years Hardy had married his secretary, Florence Dugdale, forty years his junior. He continued writing poetry until his death in 1928, having become something of a celebrity. He had refused a knighthood but accepted the Order of Merit in 1910. Hardy had wished to be buried beside Emma in Stinsford churchyard, the local church to his birthplace, but there was pressure for him to be buried in Poets' Corner in Westminster Abbey. A gruesome compromise was reached; his heart was cut out and buried at Stinsford while the rest of his body was cremated and interred in Poets' Corner.

Thomas Hardy is today regarded as one of the 'greats' of English literature. Previously novels had been funny, entertaining and romantic; they had not been a vehicle for tragedy. His stories dealt with the bleak realities and poverty of rural life and shone a light on what he perceived as the flawed values of Victorian society. His descriptions of nature and landscape are vivid and inspiring, and are still accurate to much of Dorset's countryside today.

William Barnes, 1801-1886

William Barnes was born into a farming family in the Blackmore Vale and gained fame as a writer of poems in the Dorset dialect which were first published in periodicals in the middle nineteenth century. He deserves to be remembered for much more than this however; Barnes was a true polymath, a writer, poet, priest, mathematician, artist and accomplished linguist. He became rector of St Peter's Church, Winterborne Came after studying divinity at Cambridge and is said to have been fluent in Greek, Latin, Hebrew, French, Italian, Hindi, Russian, Welsh and Old English. Before being ordained Barnes had been in charge of two schools; he was a strong advocate of removing Greek, Latin and other foreign influences from English so that it might be easier to understand for those without a classical education. Barnes was rector of St Peter's for twenty-four years and among his literary friends were Lord Tennyson, Gerard Manley Hopkins and Thomas Hardy, who visited him a number of times at the rectory in Winterborne Came.

"My Orcha'D in Linden Lea"
(extract)
'Ithin the woodlands, flow'ry gleaded,
By the woak tree's mossy moot,
The sheenen grass bleades, timber-sheaded,
Now do quiver under voot;
An' birds do whissle auver head,
An' water's bubblen in its bed,
An' ther vor me the apple tree
Do lean down low in Linden Lea.

Adam Ashley-Cooper, 1801-1885

Wimborne St Giles House is the home of the Earls of Shaftesbury. Buried in the neighbouring parish church is Adam Ashley-Cooper (1801-1885), who on his father's death, became the 7th Earl. The young Ashley-Cooper received little love and attention from his parents and recounted his days at Harrow School as particularly horrific. Luckily the family housekeeper provided the affection missing from his parents and, by all accounts, was the inspiration for his philanthropic work later on. Lord Shaftesbury entered Parliament after studying Classics at Oxford. The first humanitarian cause to attract his attention was the inhumane treatment of inmates in lunatic asylums, which he witnessed on a visit to the Bethnal Green 'madhouse'. His County Lunatic Asylums Act of 1828 ensured better, more humane care for those in such institutions. He was also instrumental in a number of Factory Acts which particularly improved conditions for women and children workers; and his Chimney Sweepers Regulation Act in 1863 put an end to young children being used as chimney sweeps. Known to many as 'the poor man's earl', thousands of poor people lined the streets of London to watch his funeral procession and the fountain and statue of Anteros, the "Angel of Christian Charity", in Piccadilly Circus were created to commemorate his philanthropic work.

Alms house, Wimborne St Giles.

More Dorset titles from Inspiring Places

All About the Jurassic Coast	£4.99
Ancient Dorset	£3.99
Explore Dorset's Churches and Abbeys	£4.99
Dorset Smugglers' Walks	£4.99
Fossils and Rocks of the Jurassic Coast	£3.99
Great Houses and Gardens of Dorset	£3.99
Guide to the Beaches and Coves of Dorset	£4.99
Walk and Explore Dorset's History	£4.99
Dorset in the World Wars	£4.99
What to See and Do in Dorset	£4.99
Jurassic Coast Fossils	£3.99
Life and Works of Thomas Hardy	£4.99
Purbeck - a brief guide	£3.99
Railway Heritage of Dorset and Somerset	£4.99
Tales of the Dorset Coast	£4.99
Dorset Teashop Walks	£4.99
The Tyneham Story	£3.99
Walk and Explore Thomas Hardy's Dorset	£3.99
Walk and Explore Mysterious Dorset	£4.99
Walking West Dorset	£4.99
Hidden Dorset	£4.99

For a full list of titles from Inspiring Places see:

www.inspiringplaces.co.uk

Photo: Bat's Head.